BREAK UP

How to move on and deal with it with a smile

THOMAS VICTORY

Table of contents

INTRODUCTION

If there's one thing I hate about love, it's uncertainty. After falling in love with someone and being happy for years, the whole relationship may fall apart. If you feel that the relationship is not working out, that's great for you. This is because you may get over your ex-boyfriend immediately after breaking up. But what if you're a sad, miserable person, crawling on the floor, crushed inside, trying to pick up pieces of your broken heart? If you are that love, love can be a real slut for you. No matter what I do, no matter how hard I try, my head is always pounding and there is a void in my heart that nothing can fill.

Because it's just pathetic. Relationships in which both lovers are separated or meet new lovers at the same time seem to be far superior to traditional breakups. But most of the time, when your lover leaves you, he may already be thinking of someone else. After all, if we're as selfish as humans, we want to have a backup plan for everything we do in life. As humans, we need purpose in everything, and we need to believe that there is something better for us, even after a breakup. But human psychology aside, the facts of the matter remain. You broke up you hurt you have to carry on It hurts, but you really don't have a choice.

Acceptance is the biggest hurdle after a breakup. Most of us are always yearning for a second chance or always hoping that our ex will come back to us. As long as you are, you will always writhe in misery and pain. And you will never be able to continue. To truly understand how to move on after a breakup, you need to be able to accept that the relationship is over. And if your ex comes back to you after a few months, you'll have to convince yourself that he's not coming back.

Living in the hope that one day your ex-boyfriend will understand how much you love and need you, especially if he starts dating someone else, day by day. I feel sick. Your willpower and determination are the only things that matter to move on after a breakup. Nothing else can help you, not your friend or problem. Stand firm, move forward, and convince yourself that you are ready to escape the pain. Then use these steps to move forward and deal with your breakup.

CHAPTER ONE

Don't write letters

I am dying to get in touch with my ex. Even when you're feeling down, listening to a romantic song, or even when you're drunk. But take that thought. Never try to get in touch with your ex-boyfriend unless you happen to meet them. It weakens your resolve to get over your ex. If you find yourself writing a long email to your ex, write it if you want, but don't send it. Please

keep this draft copy overnight.
When you wake up in the
morning, you realize it was
just a weak moment and you
don't want to send any more
emails. The longer you wait,
the stronger your resolve
becomes. The same rules
apply to calls and SMS. When
the uncontrollable urge to call
or text your ex gets the better
of you, don't hold back.
Instead, if you still want to
call, convince yourself to call

in the morning. . Every time you call or text, you feel more confident about moving on from your ex.

Deal with the addiction

Ex-boyfriends are addicted, just like any other serious life-threatening addiction in the world. And the worst part is that you can't trim a little bit at a time. The only thing you can do is go cold turkey and avoid all contact. There is none. It hurts and you feel terrible, but after a week you feel better and a week later you feel even better. Treat your ex like a bad addiction and learn to deal with the breakup.

CHAPTER TWO

Evil Selfish Ex

When your boyfriend or girlfriend dumps you, they are evil *at least in your head*. You have a right to hate him if he yells at you when he gets angry, or if he ignores you, or looks at you with malice and disgust every time you come near him... a little devil. Your ex doesn't like you anymore, he despises you. Of course, they can try to be better and more understanding. But you can't expect every ex-boyfriend to hold your hand and help you find a way out. Some ex-boyfriend likes to trip you up and kick you where it hurts...hate her. But deal with it. And get over it.

Repeat your relationship
Recreate the relationship in your mind as you sit alone and stare at a wall or an empty wine glass. Find out the flaws and weaknesses in your relationship and figure out

where the problem started. But remember to pick the flaws, not the part of the relationship. Love is over. What you need to do here is figure out what you did wrong and where your partner hurt you. Are you trying too hard to please people? And as for your ex, try to find out his faults as well so that you don't fall for another person with the same faults again.

Don't overdo it
During the first week, don't
try to convince yourself that
your ex is over. Do your best
to keep busy and get over
your ex, but don't force
yourself to forget your ex.
Though you may be able to
contain your thoughts, they
always come back out of
nowhere and hurt you even
more.

CHAPTER THREE

Be unhappy

Allow yourself to be unhappy and hurt. But time yourself and keep an eye on your calendar. It takes about three weeks to get over your ex. Mark the date on your calendar with a big red marker. During these three weeks, you'll be thinking about your ex, but remember that by the end of those three weeks, you'll be the next to wake up.

There are two kinds of fantasies to think about after a breakup. The "I wish I could go back" fantasy and the "I can count on you" fantasy. Don't post nude pics or try to do anything under the belt like that cheesy comeback. That's not fair. You can't forgive yourself for years if you have even the slightest resemblance to your conscience. Take the high road. Convince yourself that one fine day, many years from now, you can create something great out of your life by focusing your energy on other positive things.

Laugh like a crazy person
Indulge in self-pity and melancholy. But if you wake up one day and a few weeks later feel better smile! Feel your happiness. Recognize how good you feel. It will take a while, but you will feel it

when you are ready. Listen to fun songs, watch funny movies, and laugh out loud. When you are ready to get out of your sad state, your heart will be happy to help you have a good time.

CHAPTER FOUR
Curiosity and the No Contact Rule

The no-contact rule is really important. All the other stages can be used to trace all the way to the tee, but failing here will quickly return you to the drawing board. Have you checked your ex's Facebook page? When you first see your ex-girlfriend's page, you probably don't think too much about it. But as time goes on, I visit more and more of their sites until I become obsessed with the idea of wanting to learn more about my ex. Do not keep in touch or seek information to avoid it.

Better and sexier

Live your life, get out there and have fun. Sitting alone in the corner of the room doesn't make you feel any better. Date other people, or at least meet interesting dating possibilities that you like. If you find out that your ex is dating someone else, especially if he hasn't already been cheating on you with someone else Note that it is very difficult to move forward. You'll look better and the endorphins released in your body will make you feel more optimistic and look sexier. Breakups are sometimes inevitable, no matter how hard you try to prevent them. What you do next and how you pull yourself together to deal with a breakup can make the difference between someone going through a breakup and a broken lover giving up their chance to live a happy life again.

CHAPTER FIVE

Conclusion

Use these steps to move on and deal with your breakup. Following these steps may seem easy at first, but it's not as easy as it sounds.